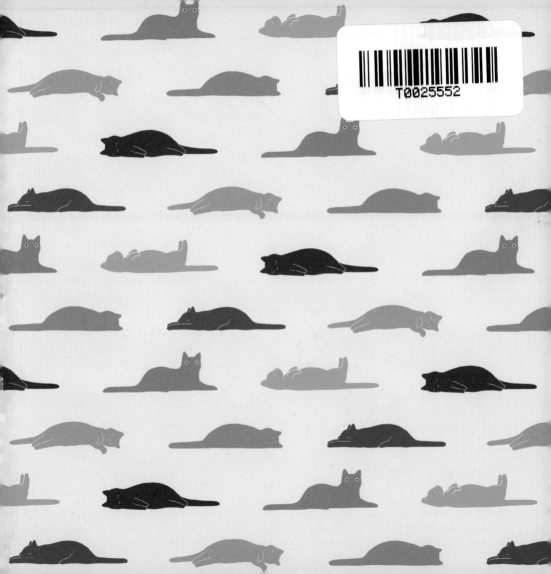

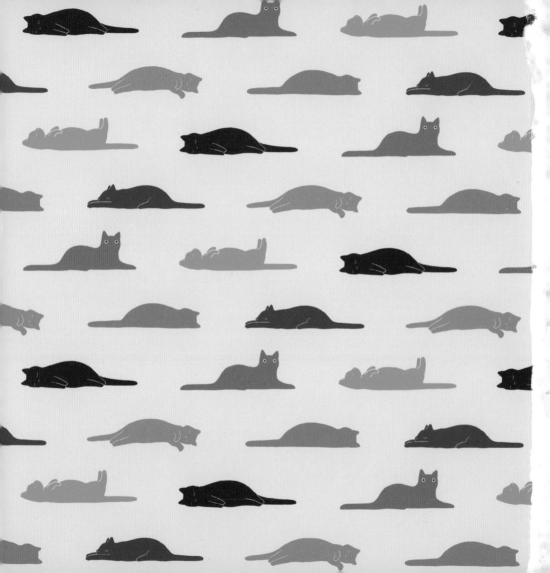

Catffirmations

Catffirmations

*Mindful Mantras to Awaken
Your Inner Cat*

ART BY Lim Heng Swee

CHRONICLE BOOKS
SAN FRANCISCO

Library of Congress Cataloging-in-Publication Data available.

ISBN 978-1-7972-1772-7

Manufactured in China.

Art by Lim Heng Swee.
Text by Marcello Picone.
Design by Evelyn Furuta.

10 9 8 7 6 5 4 3 2

CHRONICLE BOOKS
680 SECOND STREET
SAN FRANCISCO, CA 94107
WWW.CHRONICLEBOOKS.COM

I contain **multitudes**.

I am just right

just where I am.

I feel **seen**.

Abundance

comes naturally
to me.

I am calm
and confident
and
covered in
sharp spines

just in case.

I go
effortlessly
with the flow.

Now is the
perfect time

to manifest the
perfect place.

Sometimes
it's good to
let go.

I reach out

with curiosity.

I will find

my special spot

where I can be

at **peace**.

I ride the wave.
A wave that rises
with great power.

I am the wave.
A wave that crests,
knowing its direction.

I hurl free
of the wave.

I'm simply **radiant**.

If you don't
get me,
I have to go
be **awesome**
elsewhere.

I am **grounded**.

Inner peace

is just a

catnap away.

I don't have
to chase
anything
to be happy.

I am liquid.
I am stillness.
I'm a
gorgeous
contradiction.

Stress
	is not in
		my vocabulary.

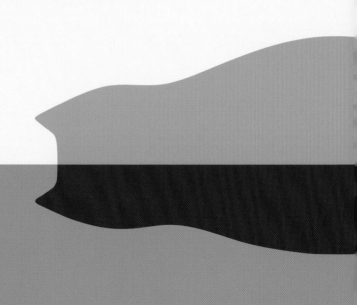

To live

is

to play.

I'm forever hanging in there.

I've had
many lives.
And I
embrace
them all.

I can
thrive
no matter
where
I am.

Life's obstacles are an **adventure**.

I leap in with sure-footed **confidence**.

And stick
the landing.

Ever **alert**.

Always **mindful**.

I'll reveal myself when I'm good and ready.

I am the **journey**.

The journey is **me**.

I **embrace** love
in my own way.

I always seek a new
perspective.

I'll know
the right time
to pounce.

I will make it to the top
on my own terms.

I can **float**

above it all.

All roads
lead to
relaxing.

Every change is an **opportunity**.

I **know** I will land on my feet.

Lean into
the eternal
flow of
time.

I.

Am.

Magnificent.

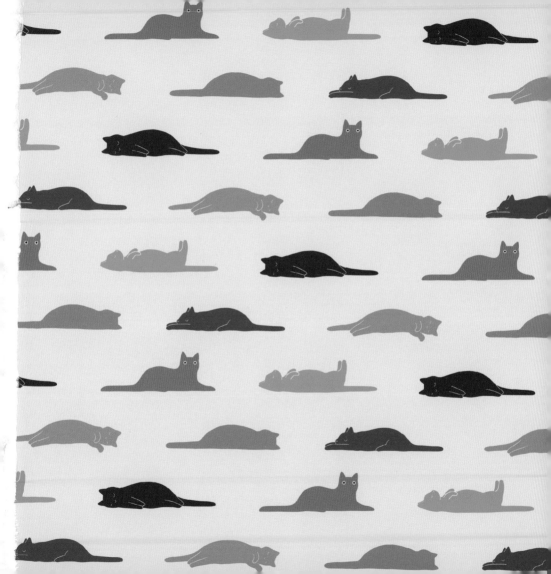

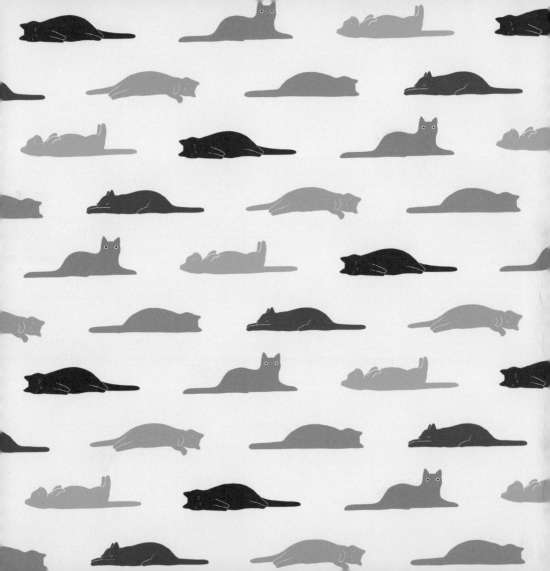